E REUBEN

The Spirit of Adoption: Embracing God as Father

First edition

This book was professionally typeset on Reedsy.
Find out more at reedsy.com

Contents

1

The Heart of the Father: Understanding God's Desire for Adoption

The sun had barely risen when Luke stood at the edge of the cliff, gazing at the horizon. His heart ached in the stillness, consumed by a deep emptiness he couldn't shake. For years, he had wandered through life, always searching for something, someone, to fill the void he felt deep inside. But nothing seemed to satisfy. His relationships were shallow, his faith distant, and his sense of purpose... lost.

The whisper of the wind in the trees seemed to beckon him, urging him to go deeper into the woods, away from the noise of the world. He followed the trail, the thorns brushing against his skin as he pressed forward, the ache in his chest growing with every step. It was as though something, or someone, was calling to him from within, inviting him to come closer. But to what? He wasn't sure.

As the trail opened into a clearing, he stumbled upon an old, weathered stone bench. It was worn with age, but still sturdy. He sat, feeling the weight of his questions pressing against him. His mind was a storm of confusion. What did it mean to be loved? To be wanted? To belong?

For years, Luke had been abandoned. His parents, absent, his friends, fleeting. He had always been the outsider. The one who didn't quite fit in. He had tried to prove his worth, tried to earn love, but every effort had only led to more rejection. Yet deep within him, a part of him longed for a love that wasn't earned but given freely. A love that wasn't based on performance but on belonging.

And it was in that moment, sitting on that stone bench in the quiet of the woods, that the answer came—soft, but unmistakable.

"Luke, you are mine. I have always wanted you."

The words pierced through his confusion like a sword of light, and he felt a sudden warmth flooding his chest. It was as if the very air around him had shifted, and he could sense the presence of something—no, someone—close by, waiting. Waiting for him to understand.

The feeling was overwhelming. It was as though the weight of all his longing, all his searching, was now being answered. There, in the stillness, he realized something profound: the love he had always sought was not something to be earned, it was a gift, and it had been there all along. But who was offering it to him? And why?

The wind picked up, rustling the leaves around him, as if echoing a deeper truth. He closed his eyes, and for the first time in his life, he felt the touch of a love that was unwavering, unconditional, and boundless. A love that didn't depend on his past or his failures, a love that simply existed for him, because he was wanted.

His heart raced as the pieces began to fall into place. There was a name for this kind of love—Father's love. The love of a parent who would never leave, never forsake. It was as if he had been adopted into a family he had never known existed, a family where he was wanted, chosen, and loved.

Luke opened his eyes, and in the distance, he saw a figure standing at the edge of the clearing, waiting. He couldn't see the person's face, but he felt their presence like a warm embrace. The figure took a step forward, and as if guided by an invisible force, Luke stood to meet them.

Before he could speak, the figure reached out, offering their hand, and said, "You are mine now. I have called you to be my own. You are my child, and I am your Father."

Luke's breath caught in his throat as the weight of the words sank in. He had always feared rejection, but in this moment, he felt more accepted, more loved than he had ever felt in his life. The walls he had built around his heart began to crumble, and for the first time, he allowed himself to believe that he was truly loved.

The figure smiled, and Luke knew. He was no longer an orphan. He was a child of God.

As the figure turned to walk away, Luke followed, feeling the weight of his new identity settling over him like a cloak of warmth. The journey was just beginning, but in his heart, he knew that he had found the love he had been searching for all along. The love of a Father who would never let him go.

The Spirit of adoption was at work, and Luke's life would never be the same.

2

From Orphan to Heir: The Journey of Transformation

The night was silent, save for the distant rustling of the trees. Luke lay awake in his bed, staring at the ceiling, his mind racing. The words the figure had spoken to him still echoed in his ears, "You are mine now. I have called you to be my own. You are my child, and I am your Father." Each time he replayed those words, a wave of emotion surged through him. Was it real? Could he truly be adopted into a family like that?

The weight of what had happened earlier in the clearing felt almost too much to bear. It was too big, too profound, to wrap his mind around all at once. But there was something undeniable about it, a truth that seeped into his very soul.

For years, Luke had wandered through life feeling like an outsider. He had never known the comfort of a loving home, a place where he could rest without fear of rejection. His childhood had been marked by loneliness, abandonment, and a constant hunger for something more. He had always been an orphan in his own eyes—untethered, unloved, forgotten. But tonight, everything had changed.

With a groan, Luke rolled over in bed, pulling the covers tightly around him. His heart pounded in his chest. He wasn't sure what to do with this newfound truth. How could he accept it? What did it even mean to be an adopted child of God?

The hours passed slowly, but eventually, he drifted into an uneasy sleep. His dreams were fragmented, filled with images of dark alleys, empty rooms, and voices calling his name. He awoke suddenly, drenched in sweat, his body trembling. It took a moment for him to remember where he was—the clearing, the figure, the words.

He sat up quickly, feeling disoriented. The night was still dark outside, but a new sense of urgency pulsed in his chest. If he was truly a child of God, there had to be something more to this journey—something that would change everything. But how?

With a sudden resolve, Luke swung his legs over the side of the bed and stood. His feet felt like lead as he walked toward the door, unsure of where he was going but certain that he couldn't stay in the quiet darkness any longer.

The streets outside were empty, the city around him still asleep. The air was cold against his skin as he walked, each step purposeful. He didn't know what he was looking for, but he knew that he had to find it. He had to understand what this adoption meant, what it would mean for his future. He couldn't shake the feeling that something was coming—a moment of clarity, or perhaps, a confrontation.

As he walked, the wind seemed to grow stronger, whipping around him like a restless spirit. He shivered, pulling his jacket tighter around himself. It was then that he saw it—an old, familiar church looming in the distance. The towering steeple stood like a beacon in the night, calling him, beckoning him toward something greater than himself. He had passed this church countless times before, but tonight, it felt different.

Without thinking, Luke quickened his pace, drawn to the building as if it were magnetic. He reached the steps and paused, looking up at the door. The heavy wooden door seemed to stand between him and whatever awaited him on the other side. Was he ready for this? Could he truly walk through it, step into a new life?

A voice, soft yet insistent, whispered inside his mind. *You are mine now. Step forward, and you will never walk alone again.*

It was the same voice from the clearing. He had no doubt now. This was God calling him, urging him to move forward into the life He had promised. Luke's breath caught in his throat as he reached for the door handle, his hand trembling.

As the door creaked open, a rush of warmth enveloped him. Inside, the church was quiet, the stained glass windows casting faint, colored light across the floor. The air smelled of incense and something ancient, sacred.

In the center of the church stood a single figure, bathed in the soft glow of the candles surrounding him. The figure turned, and for the first time, Luke saw His face—strong yet compassionate, full of love. His eyes met Luke's, and in that moment, everything that had been cloudy, uncertain, fell into place.

"I have called you, Luke. You are no longer an orphan. You are my heir," the figure said, His voice steady and warm, like a father speaking to his child.

Luke's knees buckled as the weight of the truth sank in. He had stepped from the shadows of his past into the light of a new identity. He was no longer the one searching for love. He was now the beloved son of the King. And this was just the beginning of the transformation that would change everything.

3

The Spirit of Adoption: God's Embrace Through the Holy Spirit

The morning sun had risen, casting long shadows across the floor of Luke's apartment as he sat in the stillness, unable to shake the weight of what had happened the night before. His mind buzzed with questions, and his heart beat erratically as the memory of the church lingered like an echo in his soul. He had stepped into the presence of God, heard the truth of his new identity, but something still felt incomplete.

What was he supposed to do now? How could he live as God's son? What did it mean to be adopted into His family?

Luke leaned back in his chair, staring at the small, weathered Bible that lay on the table in front of him. He had opened it several times over the past few weeks, but the words seemed distant, hard to grasp. He needed something more. He needed to understand how to move forward.

As if on cue, the words from the night before came rushing back to him: *You are mine now. You are my child, and I am your Father.*

The weight of those words still stirred something deep within him, but there was more. He had sensed it during his time in the church—the presence of something, or rather, *someone*—a presence that wasn't just God the Father, but something, someone, who had filled him with warmth and peace.

What was that?

He closed his eyes, seeking an answer. The sensation was stronger now, like a soft whisper at the back of his mind, urging him to listen. It was gentle, but persistent, like a hand reaching out, drawing him closer. He could almost hear the words clearly in his spirit.

The Spirit...

His heart skipped a beat as the realization hit him like a wave crashing against the shore. The Spirit. The Holy Spirit.

Luke stood up abruptly, feeling a new sense of urgency. He had read about the Holy Spirit in the Bible, but the truth of it had never felt so alive, so real. The Holy Spirit was the presence of God, the one who empowered believers to live as sons and daughters of the King. He was the one who made God's love tangible, the one who affirmed their identity as children of the Father.

And He was with Luke, now.

Luke's mind raced. He needed to know more. He had to understand what it meant to have the Spirit of adoption living inside him. How would it change his life? How would it change the way he saw himself?

Without thinking, Luke grabbed his coat and stepped out of the apartment. He walked with purpose, his feet carrying him toward the park where he had found himself many times before—alone, uncertain, lost. But today, it was different. Today, he was not the orphan he had once been. Today, he was a son.

The wind was cool against his face as he made his way down the path, each step heavy with anticipation. He reached the park and found a quiet bench by the small pond, the water reflecting the clear blue sky. Luke sat down, his thoughts swirling in a whirlwind.

Holy Spirit, he whispered to the air around him. *I don't understand fully, but I know you are here. Please, help me. Teach me what it means to be God's child, to live as a son of the Father. Show me how to embrace this new life.*

For a moment, there was only silence. But then, just as the breeze seemed to pick up, Luke felt a deep stirring within him—like a warmth rising from within his very being. His heart beat faster, not out of fear, but out of recognition. It was as if he were being enveloped in something far greater than himself.

And then, he felt it—a gentle, loving presence that settled around him like a blanket. It was the Holy Spirit, confirming what his heart had known all along.

I am with you. You are not alone. I will guide you, empower you, and fill you with the love of your Father.

The words didn't come through his ears, but through his spirit. They were simple, yet powerful, and they brought a peace that flooded his entire being. Luke closed his eyes, allowing the moment to wash over him, feeling the embrace of God's Spirit wrapping him in love. It was a love that was real, a love that wasn't based on performance, but on the deep, unwavering truth that he was a child of God.

For the first time in his life, Luke understood what it meant to be truly accepted. He didn't have to earn God's love. It was already his. And the Holy Spirit, God's presence within him, was the constant reminder, the constant affirmation, of that truth.

He sat there for what felt like hours, soaking in the reality of what was happening. The transformation that had begun the night before was now taking root deep in his soul.

Luke was no longer an orphan. He was a son of the King. And the Spirit of adoption was the seal, the proof, of his new identity.

As he stood to leave, he felt a newfound strength rising within him, a strength that came not from his own willpower, but from the Spirit that now lived inside him. He knew the road ahead would not always be easy, but with the Spirit's guidance, he was ready to face whatever came next.

For the first time, Luke felt at home—not in a place, but in his very being. He was not only God's child; he was His heir, and the adventure of living out that identity had just begun.

4

A New Identity: Living as a Child of God

The days that followed were a blur. Luke couldn't shake the overwhelming sense of peace that had settled over him, but at the same time, a deep uncertainty lingered. He had felt God's presence, experienced the embrace of the Holy Spirit, and had begun to understand that he was now a son of God. But what did that mean for his life? What was he supposed to do now that he knew the truth of his new identity?

It was the evening of the fourth day since his encounter in the park. Luke had been avoiding his usual distractions—work, social media, his friends who never seemed to truly understand him. For the first time in his life, he couldn't just keep running. He had to face the truth of who he was. But he didn't know where to begin.

Sitting in his small apartment, he stared at his reflection in the window. The city lights outside cast a faint glow on the glass, but it was his own face that caught his attention. Who was he now? The man who had once been an orphan, wandering through life with no direction? Or the man who had been claimed by a Father, given a new name and a new purpose?

The weight of the question pressed on him, and for a moment, he felt himself slipping back into the doubt and insecurity that had marked his past. Was it really possible to be a son of God? Could he truly live as one? He had never known anything but fear and rejection, and the thought of fully embracing this new identity seemed almost impossible.

A sudden knock on the door snapped him out of his thoughts. His heart leapt in his chest. He wasn't expecting anyone, but he walked toward the door, his steps hesitant. As he opened it, a figure stood in the hallway—a woman in her thirties, with a calm and warm demeanor.

"I'm sorry to disturb you," she said with a soft smile, "but I was wondering if I could talk to you for a moment. I'm Sarah. I live in the building next door."

Luke nodded, slightly confused but willing to listen. "Of course. What's on your mind?"

She stepped inside, and Luke noticed her eyes seemed kind, but there was something in them—something he couldn't place. She took a seat across from him, folding her hands in her lap.

"I know this may sound strange," Sarah began, her voice steady, "but I've seen something in you lately. Something different. And I couldn't ignore it."

Luke felt a wave of anxiety rush through him. "Different? I don't know what you mean."

She smiled again, her gaze gentle but direct. "It's as if there's a light inside you now. You've changed. I can feel it. It's like you've been given a new identity."

His heart skipped a beat. He had not told anyone about his encounter with God, not about his adoption as His son, or the Spirit that had filled him. How could she possibly know?

"Sarah, I..." Luke faltered, unsure how to explain. "I don't know what's happening, but you're right. Something has changed in me. I can't explain it all, but I know it's real. I feel like I've been given a new life."

Her eyes softened with understanding. "I knew it. You're not the same person anymore. It's like God has awakened something in you. I see His peace in you, Luke. It's unmistakable."

Luke stared at her, overwhelmed. "How do you know?"

She leaned forward slightly, her voice lower now, almost as if she were sharing a secret. "I've been where you are. I've had that moment of transformation. The moment when everything changes. When you realize that God isn't distant or far away, but close. That He's adopted you into His family, and your identity is no longer bound by your past. You are His child now, Luke. And nothing can take that away."

Luke felt his chest tighten. It was as if everything he had been grappling with—every question, every doubt—had just been confirmed by someone who knew, who had walked the same path.

"I've been reading the Bible," Luke confessed, his voice shaking. "But it's hard to understand. I don't know how to live this new life. I'm still so… broken."

Sarah's expression softened with compassion. "I know it's hard. It's a process. But the key is remembering who you are. You are God's son now. That changes everything. You don't have to prove yourself anymore. You don't have to earn His love. It's yours. And the Holy Spirit is there, inside you, helping you every step of the way."

Luke swallowed hard, the weight of her words sinking in. The journey ahead would not be easy. The old lies, the old fears, would still try to pull him back. But something had shifted in him. A new strength, a new hope had taken root.

"Sarah," Luke said, his voice barely above a whisper, "how do I live as God's son? How do I embrace this new identity?"

Sarah stood and placed a hand on his shoulder, her grip warm and reassuring. "You begin by accepting it. Trust in what He's done for you. And then, every day, choose to walk in that truth. Live as His son. Live as someone who has been set free, someone who is loved unconditionally. And when you stumble, remember—His grace is enough. Always."

Luke nodded, the truth of her words settling deep within him. He was no longer who he once was. He was a son of God, and it was time to step into that identity, to live it out. No matter the cost.

The journey had just begun. But Luke knew one thing for certain: he was not alone. And nothing could ever change the truth that he was God's child.

5

The Call to Courage: Facing the Darkness of the Past

The evening sky hung heavy with dark clouds as Luke walked through the narrow alleyways of the city. He hadn't been here in years, but it felt oddly familiar. The smell of rain mixed with the lingering scent of old garbage, the flicker of dim streetlights casting shadows on the walls. It was a place that had once been his refuge—the place where he hid from the world, the place where he could be invisible. But tonight, it felt different.

His footsteps echoed in the silence, each one reverberating like a drumbeat in his chest. The memories of his past, the fear, the loneliness, the desperation—those dark places he had tried to bury—came flooding back, making his heart race. He could almost hear the voices of his old life calling out to him, dragging him back into the shadows.

Luke had been trying to avoid this part of himself. Since his encounter with the Holy Spirit, he had felt a stirring in his heart—a calling to embrace his new identity, to walk as God's son, free from the chains of his past. But the fear was always lurking. The weight of old habits, old fears, was like a heavy chain, and he could feel it tightening with every step.

A figure suddenly appeared at the end of the alley, and Luke's pulse quickened. It was him. Jack. The man who had been both his tormentor and his friend, the one who had pulled him into the darkness all those years ago. Jack had always known how to manipulate Luke, how to make him feel small and weak, and for a long time, Luke had believed the lies. He had believed that he was nothing, that he didn't belong, that he was destined for failure.

Jack's eyes gleamed with recognition, and a smirk spread across his face as he took a step forward. "Well, well, well," he said, his voice low and taunting. "Look who it is. The great Luke, acting like he's better than the rest of us now."

Luke's throat tightened. He had come so far, and yet, in this moment, he felt small again, trapped in the prison of his past. The old voice inside him whispered, *You're still the same. You can't escape who you are. You'll never be good enough.*

But something else was stirring inside him now. Something stronger. The Holy Spirit, that quiet, steady presence, whispered to him in the depths of his soul, *You are not who you once were. You are mine now.*

Luke took a deep breath and stood taller, his voice steady, though his heart raced. "I'm not that person anymore, Jack."

Jack laughed, a harsh, mocking sound. "You think you can just walk away from everything? You think you can leave it all behind, like it never happened? You can't outrun your past, Luke."

The old shame surged within him, but Luke fought it back. His past didn't define him anymore. The lies he had believed for so long had no hold over him now. He was a son of God, chosen and loved, and nothing could take that away.

"I'm not running from it," Luke said, his voice firm. "I've faced my past, Jack. I've been forgiven. And I've been adopted into a new family. A family that loves me. A family that calls me their own."

Jack's expression faltered for a moment, and Luke could see the doubt flash in his eyes. But then the smirk returned, colder than before. "You think you're better than me now, huh? Just because you've found some new religion? You think that makes you better than everyone else?"

Luke shook his head. "It's not about being better, Jack. It's about being healed. I don't need to live in shame anymore. I don't need to prove anything. I'm loved just as I am."

For a moment, there was silence between them, the tension palpable. Luke's heart pounded, but he felt a strange calm rising within him. The weight of his past, the guilt, the shame—he wasn't carrying it anymore. It had been taken from him. And now, it was time to stand firm in the truth of who he was.

Jack's face twisted with anger, but Luke didn't flinch. He knew the battle wasn't over, but the victory had already been won.

"You'll see, Luke," Jack spat, turning to walk away. "You'll be back. You always come crawling back."

Luke stood there, watching him disappear into the darkness. His hands trembled, but the quiet strength of the Holy Spirit surged within him, anchoring him in the truth of God's love. For the first time, he felt the weight of his past fully lifting, as if the chains that had once bound him were falling away.

Luke took a deep breath, his chest rising and falling with the rhythm of his new life. He wasn't the same man he had been. His identity was no longer defined by fear, by shame, by the brokenness of his past. He was God's son now, and nothing—nothing—could take that away.

As he turned and walked back down the alley, the city lights flickered ahead of him. The path ahead would not always be easy. But with the Holy Spirit guiding him, Luke knew that he was not alone. He had been called out of darkness and into the light of his Father's love. And no matter what came next, he would never walk that path alone again.

6

The Battle Within: Confronting the Lies

Luke woke to the sharp sound of his phone buzzing on the nightstand. Groggily, he reached for it, squinting at the screen. It was a message from Sarah.

"Luke, I've been praying for you. The enemy will try to make you doubt your identity in Christ. Don't let him win. You are God's child, and that's your truth. Trust in His strength, not your own."

Luke stared at the words, a sense of unease creeping through him. It wasn't the message that unsettled him—it was the timing. The night before, he had finally felt like he was standing firm in his new identity as a son of God. The weight of his past, the fear that had bound him for so long, had seemed to lift, and for the first time, he felt free.

But now, as he sat up in bed and wiped the sleep from his eyes, something inside him stirred, something dark, like a shadow creeping in from the corners of his mind. The peace he had felt only hours before began to slip away, replaced by a gnawing uncertainty.

He ran his hands through his hair and stood up, trying to shake off the discomfort. He needed to get out, to clear his head. It was early, but the stillness of the morning was something he had always cherished.

As he stepped into the shower, the sound of the water cascading over him did little to ease the tension building in his chest. His thoughts circled back to his conversation with Jack in the alley, the venom in Jack's words still echoing in his mind. *You'll be back. You always come crawling back.*

Luke gripped the shower wall, his breath coming faster as the weight of those words pressed down on him. Jack's voice wasn't just in his head anymore; it was louder now, more insistent. *You don't belong. You're still the same broken person. You can't escape who you are.*

The sound of the water seemed to amplify the negative thoughts swirling in his mind. Luke closed his eyes, trying to calm his racing heart, but it was as though something inside him was fighting for control. He wasn't the same person anymore. He *knew* that. But the battle between what he knew and what he felt was tearing him apart.

He stepped out of the shower, shivering despite the warmth of the bathroom. The room seemed to close in on him, the familiar space now feeling suffocating. His phone buzzed again, breaking the silence.

Another message from Sarah.

"Luke, remember, the enemy's lies are loud, but God's truth is louder. His love is greater than any doubt."

Luke's hands shook as he read her words. He wanted to believe them, but the shadows inside him were growing stronger, whispering louder with every passing second. The lies were starting to feel like his own thoughts, his own voice, and it was becoming harder to distinguish them from the truth.

Without thinking, he grabbed his coat and left the apartment, heading for the park. The crisp morning air hit his face, sharp and cold, but it didn't seem to clear the fog clouding his mind. He walked quickly, hoping the physical movement would help drown out the noise inside his head, but it only grew louder.

You're not worthy of God's love. You'll never be enough. You can't change who you are.

Luke stopped in the middle of the park, his breath coming in ragged gasps. He closed his eyes, trying to shut out the voices, but they only grew more insistent. *The Holy Spirit isn't really with you. You're alone. You've always been alone.*

The weight of the thoughts nearly crushed him. He wanted to cry out, to scream, but no sound escaped his lips. He felt paralyzed, trapped by the lies that now felt like chains around his soul.

And then, in the stillness of the moment, he heard it. A voice—soft but unmistakable.

Luke, you are not alone.

His eyes snapped open, his pulse quickening as he glanced around. The park was empty, save for a few distant figures walking along the path. But there was no one close enough to have spoken.

Luke, you are mine. You are my son. I have never left you.

The voice was calm, gentle, but full of authority. It was the voice of truth—the truth that he had felt in his spirit, the truth that had changed him. Luke's heart pounded as the weight of those words settled over him like a blanket. The lies still raged within him, but they were fading, shrinking, their power dissipating in the face of God's voice.

"I am Yours," Luke whispered, barely believing the words himself.

You are my son, and I am with you. Stand firm in this truth. The battle is not yours to fight alone. I have already won.

The weight lifted from his shoulders, and for the first time in what felt like forever, Luke felt the peace that had eluded him return, stronger than before. The lies were still there, lurking in the background, but they no longer had power over him. He was a son of God, and nothing—nothing—could change that truth.

He took a deep breath, the air filling his lungs with a new sense of purpose. He wasn't alone. The battle was real, but God's truth was greater than any doubt or fear. And with that truth, Luke knew he could face whatever came next.

He turned and walked back toward the city, the weight of his past finally behind him. The journey was far from over, but for the first time, Luke was confident that he could walk it with his Father by his side.

7

The Test of Faith: A Friend in Need

The world felt different to Luke now—brighter, clearer, more purposeful. Yet, as he stood outside the coffee shop where he had arranged to meet Sarah, a wave of doubt crept in. He wasn't sure why; the friendship between him and Sarah had been a source of strength since that first conversation in his apartment. She had been a constant reminder of the truth God had revealed to him. But today was different. He could feel it in his bones. There was a storm brewing, one that he wasn't sure he was ready for.

He glanced at his watch. She was late, but that wasn't unusual. Sarah often ran late, a habit he had learned to accept. He found a seat by the window and gazed out at the street. The city bustled with life, but Luke felt as though he were in a bubble, disconnected from the world around him. His thoughts wandered to his own struggle. Though he had found peace in God's truth, there were moments—like this one—when it seemed as if the shadows of his past were right on the edge of his consciousness, ready to pull him back.

Suddenly, the door opened, and Sarah stepped inside, looking flustered. She spotted Luke immediately and made her way toward him, her face pale.

"Hey, sorry I'm late," she said, sliding into the seat across from him. "I've had a crazy morning."

Luke raised an eyebrow, sensing something was off. "What happened? You look like you've seen a ghost."

She hesitated for a moment, her eyes darting around the coffee shop before meeting his. "It's my brother, Luke," she said quietly. "He's in trouble."

Luke's heart skipped a beat. Sarah's family was something she rarely talked about, and when she did, it was always with a certain distance. Her relationship with her brother had always been strained, and for her to mention him now, in such a way, spoke volumes.

"What kind of trouble?" Luke asked, leaning forward, his instincts on high alert.

"He's mixed up with some dangerous people," she replied, her voice trembling. "People who don't play by the rules. I don't know the full details, but I'm scared for him. And, Luke, I'm scared for me, too."

Luke's mind raced. "What do you mean? How are you involved?"

She looked down at the table, her fingers nervously tapping against her coffee cup. "I... I've been trying to help him. I've been talking to him, praying for him, but every time I think he's turning a corner, he falls deeper. And now... now, these people are threatening me, Luke. They're saying if I don't stay out of it, they'll hurt him. Hurt me." She paused, looking up at him with wide eyes. "I don't know what to do."

A cold shiver ran down Luke's spine. This was a far cry from the calm, peaceful conversations they had shared in the past weeks. There was real danger here. And Sarah wasn't just asking for advice—she was looking for a lifeline.

Luke's mind flashed back to the battle within himself—the doubt, the fear, the voices that told him he wasn't strong enough. He had fought those battles, but this was different. This was someone else's fight, and it was now pulling him into the storm.

Sarah reached across the table, her hand trembling as she grasped his. "Luke, I don't know who else to turn to. Can you help me? Can you pray with me?"

He felt a surge of empathy but also fear. He had never been in a situation like this before. His new identity as God's son had been a personal revelation, something that had radically changed his life. But could he really stand in the gap for someone else, someone in such real danger? The weight of the responsibility pressed down on him.

But then, he remembered the promises he had heard—the promises of God's faithfulness, His provision, and His power to overcome any darkness. He wasn't alone. He was never alone. And in that moment, something shifted inside him. This wasn't just about Sarah's brother; this was a test of his faith.

Luke squeezed her hand. "I'll help you," he said, his voice more confident than he felt. "We'll face this together. I don't have all the answers, but I know one thing: God is with us. And He's greater than any darkness we're facing."

Tears welled up in Sarah's eyes as she nodded, grateful but still terrified. "I don't know what I would do without you, Luke. I feel like I'm drowning."

"You're not alone, Sarah," Luke said firmly. "You never will be again. We'll pray. We'll trust that God will make a way."

Luke closed his eyes, taking a deep breath as he reached for the peace he had learned to rely on. This wasn't just about confronting the lies in his own life anymore; it was about standing firm in God's truth and authority, even when the world felt like it was crashing down around him.

As he prayed, a deep sense of calm settled over him. He felt the weight of the situation, but he also felt the presence of God, steady and sure. This was the moment he had been waiting for—the moment to prove to himself that God's power was greater than anything, that He could be trusted, no matter the circumstances.

When Luke opened his eyes, he felt different. Stronger. More certain. "We're going to get through this," he said, meeting Sarah's gaze with unwavering faith. "Together."

And as they walked out of the coffee shop, ready to face whatever lay ahead, Luke knew that this was the test of his faith he had been preparing for. The battle would be hard, but he wasn't walking it alone.

8

The Darkened Doorway: A Choice of Consequence

The night was unusually still, the kind of silence that wraps itself around you and weighs on your chest. Luke stood at the threshold of an unfamiliar house, the dim porch light flickering above him. The door was slightly ajar, as if waiting for him. He hadn't been here before, and the air surrounding the house felt thick—like it had been holding secrets for years.

He glanced at Sarah, who stood beside him, her face drawn with worry. Her hand trembled slightly as it rested against the cold doorframe. She had been quiet since they left the coffee shop, the weight of the situation pressing heavily on her shoulders. This was it—the place where they hoped to confront the danger that loomed over her brother. But everything inside Luke screamed that this wasn't just any house. There was something about it that felt wrong, something in the atmosphere that made his pulse race and his stomach churn.

"Are you sure about this?" Luke asked, his voice barely more than a whisper.

Sarah nodded, her jaw clenched. "I have to do this. For him."

Luke didn't respond. He didn't have the words. He could see the fear in Sarah's eyes, the same fear that had been gnawing at him since she first shared her brother's situation. The shadows of danger were closing in, and they had no choice but to confront them head-on. Still, every instinct within him told him to turn away. To walk back into the safety of the known world. But the Holy Spirit within him urged him forward. He couldn't deny it any longer: this was a test of his trust.

The door creaked open wider, and they stepped inside, the smell of must and stale air hitting them like a wall. Luke felt a coldness, a sense of being watched, though he saw no one. The darkness inside the house seemed to swallow them whole. His heart pounded as he followed Sarah through the narrow hallway, the floorboards groaning under their weight. The house was silent, save for the soft rustling of leaves against the windows.

Sarah led the way, her footsteps light but deliberate. She stopped in front of a closed door at the end of the hallway and turned to Luke, her face pale, lips trembling.

"This is it," she whispered. "He's in there. But... he's not alone. I don't know who else is with him."

Luke's mind raced. This wasn't just about rescuing her brother anymore. Something much darker was at play. He could feel it—like a weight pressing down on the house, suffocating it. The voices of doubt and fear whispered in his ear, urging him to back away. But this wasn't a time to be weak. He had to stand firm. They had to face the darkness, no matter how terrifying it might be.

Without another word, Sarah opened the door. The room was dimly lit, the only source of light coming from a flickering lamp in the corner. Sarah's brother, Mark, sat in the center of the room, his face bruised, his body bruised, but his eyes were wide with something more terrifying than the physical pain.

Around him, several shadowy figures stood, watching them with unreadable expressions. Their faces were obscured in the dim light, but their presence filled the room, thick and oppressive. Luke felt his heart skip a beat as one of the figures turned slowly toward him. It was as if the entire room had become a cage, and they were trapped in it.

"Sarah," Mark rasped, his voice rough with fear. "I told you not to come. You don't understand... these people... they won't stop. They don't care who you are. They don't care what you believe."

The air seemed to grow colder as the figure nearest to Mark took a step forward. Luke's breath caught in his throat. The man was tall, with dark, hollow eyes that seemed to pierce through him. He smiled—a slow, chilling smile that made Luke's blood run cold.

"You should listen to your brother, little girl," the man said, his voice smooth, almost mocking. "You've stepped into something you don't understand. There's no way out now."

Luke's stomach twisted. There was a heaviness in the air, a sense of finality. This wasn't just a confrontation about Sarah's brother anymore. This was something much more sinister. The man's words were dripping with dark intent, and Luke realized with sudden clarity that they weren't just after Mark—they were after *all* of them.

Sarah's hand squeezed Luke's arm, her grip tight with fear, but also determination. "We can't let them win. We have to get Mark out of here."

Luke nodded, his mind racing. He wasn't sure what they were up against, but the one thing he knew for certain was that they couldn't leave without a fight. The Spirit inside him surged, filling him with a boldness he had never felt before.

He stepped forward, his voice steady but resolute. "In the name of Jesus, we command you to leave this place. You have no power here."

For a moment, the room was silent. The figure in front of them stared, his smile vanishing, replaced by an expression of confusion—and then anger.

"You dare—?" the man began, but before he could finish, the lamp flickered violently, its light almost blinding.

The tension in the room shattered, and for the first time, Luke felt an undeniable surge of strength. The darkness was real, but God's power was greater.

Suddenly, the figure lunged toward them, but before he could reach them, the door slammed shut with a deafening crash. Luke's heart raced. They weren't alone, but they weren't powerless either. They had a choice to make.

And with every ounce of faith, Luke knew that the fight had only just begun.

9

The Unseen Enemy: A Whisper in the Dark

The door slammed shut behind them with an eerie finality. The air in the room grew heavy, thick with a pressure that made it feel impossible to breathe. Luke stood frozen for a moment, his eyes darting around the dimly lit room. The flickering lamp cast long, twisted shadows on the walls, stretching unnaturally. The figures that had once been a vague presence now surrounded them, closing in, their faces still hidden, their intentions unclear.

Sarah's breath came in sharp, ragged gasps as she clung to Luke's side. Her grip tightened, and Luke could feel the pulse in her hand, rapid and frantic. Her brother Mark sat on the floor, still bound to the chair, his face pale and streaked with blood. But his eyes—his eyes were full of a deep, consuming fear.

"Luke... they won't stop," Mark whispered, his voice hoarse. "They'll tear us apart if we stay here."

Luke's pulse raced as the oppressive darkness seemed to press in on him from all sides. The man who had smiled so menacingly earlier stood at the far side of the room, his silhouette a dark outline against the flickering light. The others—still as shadows—moved in a circle around them, making no sound. Their silence was far more unsettling than any words could have been.

"They're not just after Mark," Sarah whispered, her voice trembling. "They want us both. They're not... they're not human. They can't be."

Luke felt the weight of her words sink into him. He had known there was something unnatural about this situation, something more sinister than he had imagined. But hearing Sarah's fear, hearing her confirmation of his own suspicions, only made the weight heavier. These were no ordinary criminals—they were something darker, something ancient.

The man at the far side of the room smiled again, though it was a smile without humor. "You think you can just walk in here, pray, and walk out untouched?" His voice was low, mocking, and it sent a chill through Luke's spine. "You are far out of your depth. There is no way out. Not for you. Not for her."

Luke swallowed hard, feeling the weight of the situation settle in. But then, something stirred within him—the same quiet, unwavering confidence he had felt before. The voice of the Spirit, firm and clear, whispered through the chaos: *You are not alone. Stand firm.*

He took a step forward, forcing the words to come, even as his heart pounded in his chest. "In the name of Jesus, I command you to leave. This place, this darkness—it has no hold here."

For a moment, the room seemed to hold its breath, as if everything stopped, waiting. Then, the figure in the corner laughed—a deep, guttural sound that seemed to vibrate through the walls, through Luke's bones.

"You have no idea what you're dealing with," the man said, his voice growing more distorted. "This is no place for your prayers. This is our domain. And now you will witness true power."

The temperature in the room dropped dramatically, and Luke felt his breath catch. It was as though the very air had turned to ice. The shadows seemed to pulse and shift, forming into shapes that defied reason—twisting and contorting, moving toward them like a living entity.

Luke's heart raced, but he didn't move. He knew what he had to do.

He reached out, grasping Sarah's trembling hand. Her eyes met his, wide with fear, but also with something else—an unspoken plea for hope.

"Stay with me," he said quietly, his voice steady despite the terror building in the room. "God is with us. He won't leave us."

But the man stepped forward, his eyes narrowing, and his mouth twisted into a cruel smile. "You think you can defeat us with your faith? Your pathetic prayers? You are weak, just like the rest of them."

Suddenly, one of the shadows lunged toward them, and Luke's heart stopped. His body reacted before his mind could catch up. He reached out, his hand instinctively raised, and in that moment, he felt it—the surge of divine power flowing through him like a torrent of light. His fingers tingled with energy as the words of authority flowed from his lips.

"Leave this place, in Jesus' name!"

The shadow screeched as if in pain, its form disintegrating into thin air. The others hesitated for a split second, but then the laughter started again—louder, angrier, echoing off the walls.

"You think you've won?" The voice of the leader twisted and contorted, becoming unrecognizable, filled with venom. "You think you're strong? We are eternal. You will fall."

The shadows moved again, this time more violently, charging toward them like a flood. Luke's pulse quickened as he realized the enemy was not retreating—they were coming for him with greater force than before.

But then, in the midst of the chaos, Sarah's voice broke through. "We won't fight alone," she cried out, her voice strong despite the terror. "We're not alone!"

As if in response, Luke felt the air shift—like a wave crashing over him, overwhelming and powerful. The darkness shrank back, recoiling from the sudden light that filled the room. It was a presence so overwhelming that it pushed the shadows into retreat. The very walls seemed to hum with the power of God's presence.

The leader's face twisted in fury. "No! This is not how it ends!"

But the light only grew stronger, blinding them, and in the next instant, the shadows disappeared.

Luke's breathing was ragged as the room fell silent. The oppressive weight lifted, and he realized his knees were trembling. But he wasn't alone. Sarah's hand was still in his, and Mark's fearful eyes were filled with something else now—hope.

The enemy had retreated—for now.

Luke exhaled, his heart still racing. The battle wasn't over. But for the first time, he felt certain of one thing: they had won a victory. And that victory had only been possible because they had not fought alone.

10

The Revelation: A Promise Fulfilled

The house was silent, but Luke's heart was anything but calm. The oppressive darkness had receded, but its presence still lingered in the air like a shadow waiting to strike again. He stood at the center of the room, his breath shallow, his mind racing. He had no idea how long they had been there—minutes, hours? Time seemed to have stretched and contracted in that space, but now, as the adrenaline began to fade, the reality of their situation settled in.

Sarah stood beside him, her eyes wide, her body trembling. She hadn't spoken a word since the shadows had vanished, but Luke could see the mix of awe and fear on her face. Her brother Mark, still bound to the chair, looked just as stunned. His usual defiance was gone, replaced with something more fragile—an exhaustion that ran deep.

"Is it over?" Mark whispered hoarsely, his eyes darting nervously toward the corners of the room as though expecting the shadows to return at any moment.

Luke glanced around, his pulse still quick. "I don't know," he murmured. The light from the flickering lamp cast strange shadows across the walls, but the room felt... different now. Lighter, somehow. He had prayed with everything he had, and the power of God had surged through him in a way he had never experienced before. But he knew that what they had faced was not the end. It had only been the beginning.

The stillness stretched between them like a taut wire, waiting to snap.

Suddenly, the door to the room creaked open.

Luke's heart leaped into his throat. His body tensed as he instinctively stepped in front of Sarah and Mark, preparing himself for another attack. But it wasn't one of the dark figures that entered the room—it was a man.

Tall, with graying hair and a worn face, he stepped inside, his presence commanding. He looked at Luke with eyes full of knowing, as though he had been watching them for some time. A quiet understanding passed between them before he spoke.

"You've done well," the man said, his voice low and steady, yet carrying a weight of authority. "But there is much more to this than you know."

Luke blinked, confusion washing over him. He had never seen this man before. "Who are you?" he asked, trying to steady his racing heartbeat.

The man smiled faintly. "A friend. Or, perhaps more accurately, a guide." He walked toward them, his footsteps slow but purposeful. "You've faced the darkness that surrounds Sarah's brother. But the true danger lies elsewhere."

Luke's brow furrowed as he glanced at Sarah, whose eyes were filled with uncertainty. Mark, too, was looking at the man, his mouth slightly open, as if unsure whether to trust him.

"The darkness you've encountered tonight," the man continued, "was just a glimpse of something far older, far more dangerous than you realize. This isn't about just Mark or Sarah. This is a battle that stretches beyond what you can see with your eyes."

Luke's stomach dropped. A cold sensation crept over him as he processed the man's words. "What do you mean? What kind of battle?"

The man's eyes shifted to Sarah, then back to Luke. "It's a spiritual war. One that has been waged for centuries. The forces you've confronted tonight are part of something much larger, something that has been pulling at your lives in unseen ways." He paused, studying Luke's reaction. "You were chosen for this. Not just for Sarah, but for what's coming next."

Luke swallowed hard. He had always known that his journey with God was more than just a personal transformation. But now, it felt as though the weight of destiny was pressing down on him. His mind spun with questions, but the man continued, his voice unwavering.

"There is a power at work here," the man said, his eyes darkening. "A force that wants to twist the truth and bring the world into chaos. It has taken root in the hearts of many, and those you faced tonight are only its foot soldiers. But its true leaders—those who pull the strings—they are still hidden, watching."

Luke's breath caught in his throat as he felt the magnitude of the situation unfolding before him. His chest tightened with an overwhelming sense of urgency. "What do we do now?" he asked, his voice barely above a whisper.

The man studied him, his gaze intense. "You keep fighting. Not with your strength, but with God's. You have His power, Luke. Don't forget that. He will guide you. He will protect you. But you must stay vigilant, because the enemy will not rest."

For a moment, the room seemed to pulse with the weight of his words. The light from the lamp flickered again, casting long shadows across the floor. Luke glanced at Sarah, who was standing motionless beside him, her face pale but resolute.

"Stay vigilant," she repeated softly, as if testing the words, finding their strength.

The man turned to leave, his steps echoing softly as he moved toward the door. "The battle is far from over," he said, his voice fading. "But remember this: You are never alone. Not as long as you stand in the light."

And then, he was gone.

Luke stood in the center of the room, the silence once again pressing in around them. But this time, it was different. He wasn't alone. He felt the weight of the promise, the truth of God's presence with him, stronger than ever before.

"We're not alone," he whispered to Sarah, his voice firm with conviction. "And we won't be until this is finished."

They stood together, facing the unknown, but no longer in fear. The road ahead was uncertain, the battles yet to come were dark and dangerous, but in that moment, Luke knew one thing for certain: they would face them with God by their side. And that made all the difference.

The storm was far from over, but they were ready.

www.ingramcontent.com/pod-product-compliance
Ingram Content Group UK Ltd.
Pitfield, Milton Keynes, MK11 3LW, UK
UKHW020214270125
454178UK00010B/560

9 788025 327234